Author Dedication

I dedicate this book to life and family. To the
trials and tribulations I've been through and
lessons learned. To the people that we're used to
mold a better me. To the people that encouraged
and inspired me. To my ram in the bush, my
husband. Although God could have used anyone
to truly introduce Christ in my life he used you
and I'm so grateful that he did. We've weathered
a lot of storms and we did it holding on to one
another. I've never taken you or your love for me
and our children for granted or your hard work.
God ordained the right man for the right woman. I
love you and pray that God continues to bless you
on this journey called life.

Troyal Tillman

Table of Context

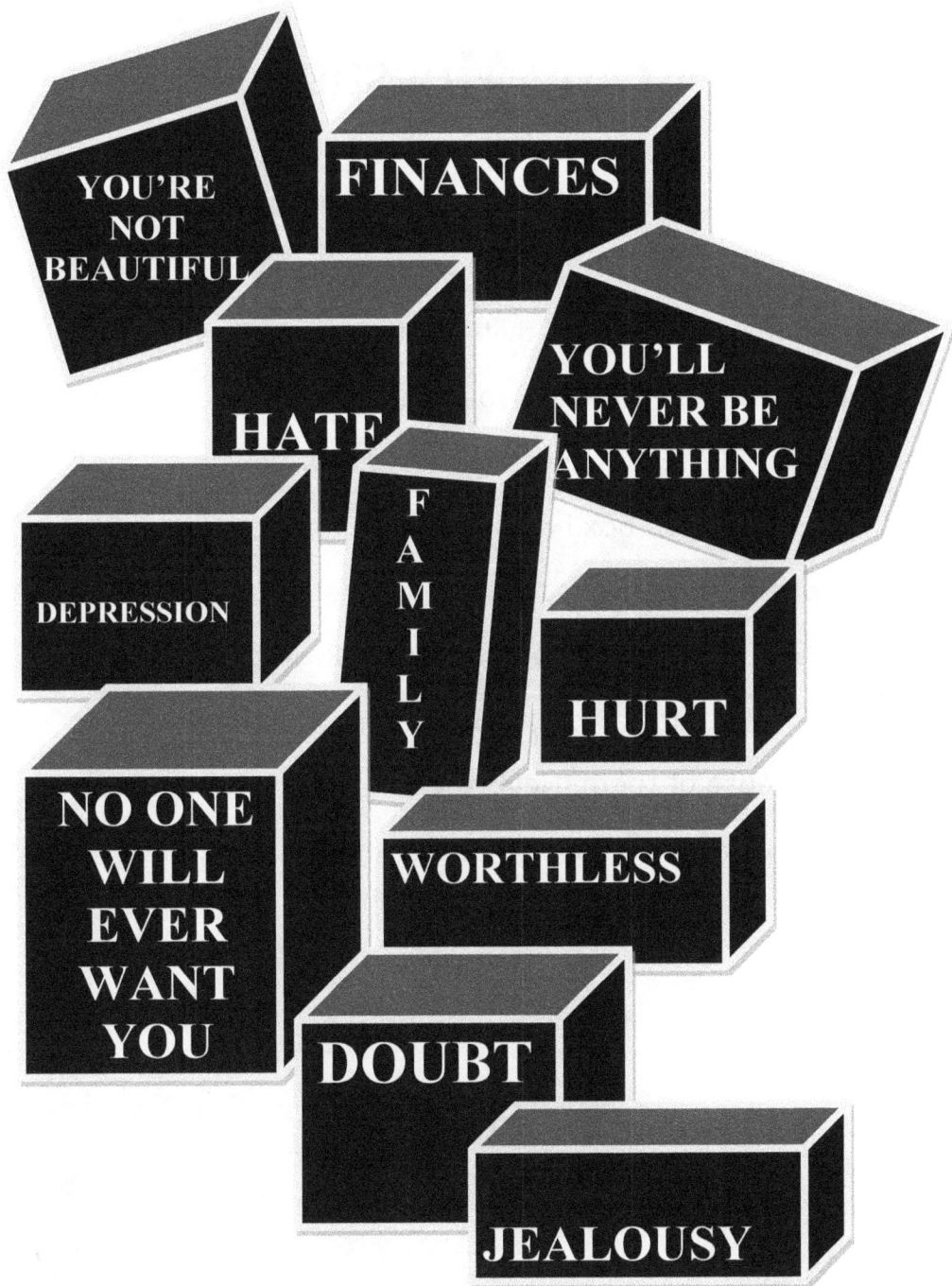

Opening Message

These are just a few hurtful words and things that can be used to tear you down or that you can go through during life. It is impossible for negativity to uplift you to walk into your purpose and it will hold you hostage. Time for you to gain access to POWER. Power that will allow you to take all the burdens that each box holds and use them to stand on to reach the plateau you're meant to be on. You are called to be GREAT in God, who gives you the POWER. Negative things have held me back for a very long time and I've thought less of myself because of them. Nevertheless, I discovered there's strength in pain and hurt. If God allows something to transpire in your life you will overcome it.

"For I reckon that the sufferings of this present time are not worthy to be compared with the glory which shall be revealed in us."

Romans 8:18 KJV

Hate

Hate is a very strong thing. Hate can not only destroy others but it will destroy you even more. When you carry something so heavy with you it takes a toll on your mind, body, and spirit. If you aren't careful you will find yourself consumed with the thoughts of others. Hate easily sneaks in, it can start with a simple judgement. Once you take the time to judge someone Satan shows you how incompatible they are with you and he uses it as a tactic. He tends to sneak in thoughts about that individual little by little and then you start to judge more and then pick out everything they are doing and eventually anything they do you find fought in it and by than hate has already taken over. If you proclaim to be a child of God you cannot hate someone for what they have done to you or someone else. God has called us to love with an agape love. So, no matter what anyone does your reaction should always be of love and not hate. Don't allow hate to keep you burden down at all. It will hold you captive and have your purpose and soul lost forever.

"He that saith he is in the light, and hateth his brother, is in darkness even until now. He that loveth his brother abideth in the light, and there is none occasion of stumbling in him".
1 John 2:9-10

"Let all bitterness, and wrath, and anger, and clamour, and evil speaking, be put away from you, with all malifce: and be ye kind one to another,

tenderhearted, forgiving one another, even as God for

Christ's sake hath forgiven you."

Ephesians 4:31-32

"Hatred stirreth up strifes: but love covereth all sins."

Proverbs 10:12

"But I say unto you which hear, Love your enemies, do

good to them which hate you,Bless them that curse

you, and pray for them which despitefully use you."

Luke 6:27-28

Family

I struggled with understanding the purpose of family since I married my husband. You're probably saying how can a woman who's married with children not understand the point of family. Well I'll tell you. In my family growing up I had a mother and father physically there, but was always told I don't have to do nothing for you, you should be happy that I put a roof over your head and feed you. There was no true togetherness. The moments we did have together was with my mother who was boggled down with the trials and tribulations in her marriage and the world. I've known them to work and fight. When it came to involvement with the children it was pretty much non-existent. My dad did his thing, he worked, he was the cook in our house when food was cooked, otherwise we ate "air pudding". My dad hung out with his friends at home, in the streets, and clubs and when home, he mainly slept or stayed outside drinking his brown liquor listening to music.

My mother was a hard worker and we went to church on Sundays at first because it was important to her but later it felt more like a routine. There was a time as a child it appeared to me that her commitment to Christ seem to shine through and she would by herself make us read on our own and we would gather together and talk about what we read but that didn't last long at all. It felt like I witnessed the more she tried holding on to her marriage and relating to my father her relationship with God changed. My sibling and I were more so pitted against one another on some level, rather than told to love, hang on to one another, and support each other. But when it came to fighting we were told to fight, if one fought and my dad found out that the other siblings didn't fight, whether winning or losing he would beat our butts.

-When Two Become One-

Story of the past

For me my husband was my ram in the bush. I was struggling in my life. I was in another city as a child living the life of an adult trying to juggle two jobs and a full schedule in college. I couldn't do everything because it was too much and the way I figured things out, it was more important to have a place to stay and food to eat, so I eventually dropped out of college with two semesters left because I had convinced myself that I needed a break and I would go back. The the job I was working wasn't getting all my bills paid and I was struggling more with absolutely no help from my family. I had a little help from my boyfriend at the time (my husband). I can clearly remember driving in my car leaving the daiquiri shop about to get a little tipsy to get enough courage to go into this strip club. I started to drive down the road and head to the local strip club because I was tired of not making it. I wasn't saved but I heard a voice as if a person was sitting next to me, if you go there and sign up your life will never be the same and a picture flashed in my head of a woman in battered struggling down the main highway drunk and on drugs. I was shown I was going to be a drug addict and drunk and I would never have a chance to get out of the mess I was headed in. I was told there's better ahead if I just hold on, change is coming. Although I didn't have a relationship with God I trusted the voice I heard and I turned around and went to my apartment and not even two weeks later my boyfriend (who I was on done with completely) called me and we worked things out and got on a better track. Soon after getting on a better track we decided to move in with each other, he consulted with his dad about the move before we moved in with each other. The conversation between them made him really think and he valued me and his soul enough to know that he wanted to do things right. So, we decided to get married and then the door opened for me to get to know Jesus and truly accept him and my life hasn't been the same.

A time that was supposed to be joyous and full of love, was pretty much a time of mourning for me. Everything to discourage me from marrying my husband was told to me and not because he was a bad individual or not good for me. Their reasoning was, they didn't think I was ready. I ultimately think that some didn't know why they were against it and some just was upset because they were losing the control they had over me. Someone went to the extent of faking a heart attack. You probably say, NO, how can someone fake a heart attack. Well let's just say if a person is having a heart attack they don't tend to drive themselves to the hospital. Let alone drive to a hospital that's 45 minutes away when the nearest one was 10 minutes away. My father fought me the entire time and my mother had to force him to get dressed and when we road to the church he tried talking me out. All that everyone was doing you would think I was marrying a killer. But I was marrying the most loving kindest guy to me I've ever known, not to mention he had then chosen to have a made up mind about Christ and live a righteous life.

Satan planted seeds in every persons' mind to interpreted the plan God had called for me to walk in. Because of a unfamiliar voice I heard weeks back I stayed firm in my decision to changed and do better in life. Everyone isn't going to understand the path you're going to take. The path is yours and you must remain firm. Some will get upset, some will accuse you of thinking you're better than them, and will fight against you without reasoning. Although I had just married my soulmate I felt abandoned and without support and once again not accepted. I continued to stick with Christ and stayed on course because I felt something on the inside say stay the course! Something telling me I was going to be blessed because of my obedience.

Transitions in life are sometimes hard, this phase was for me and left a heavy weight. I started to really feel alone and I didn't feel embraced, or wanted by anyone. Marrying into a new family the pressure was on me to open up and value them. Which made me really close myself off and I begin to feel Closter phobic. I was no longer able to be myself, leaving me to believe as if they were the privilege and I was the pion.

So I was left with no safe place, no mother I could talk too, no father that would cover me. I pretty much felt disown and talked about by my entire family. I had no peace of mind nor was I able to trust people and believe in family. I was then left with the notion that everyone had a selfish motive and if I couldn't be of assistance I was useless. Satan had me wondering, what's the point of family? If the people who God gave me directly as family who I share the same blood with can quickly disown you and cast you down when you're trying to better your life, then what's the point. I didn't focus much on my husband's family because I didn't believe I was part of their family.

I tell you this because although my family didn't understand what was going on and Satan used them all to fight what God had in store for me, I listened to the voice I heard and step out on faith when I didn't know what faith was and received the ultimate blessing. I got to know Christ for myself. But I also allowed Satan to plant the seed of discard between me and my family which left a box of distrust and hurt on me in my saved life but I have chosen to take that box marked family that was full of hurt and discard and evil and I decided to use it as a building block for myself to get closer to God rather than a burden that causes my flesh to hold hate in my heart which ultimately stops me from entering heaven. This box held me down and its marked FAMILY and it was filled with lots of barriers, hurt, resentment, no self-worth, or understanding of family and real love. I've come to realize that if I had no one God is my father, he is my everything. When you need that earthly family to be there, know that he has provided you with a great spiritual family.

Know that everything that happens to you is for your good. Even when it involves people that's closest to you. God always provides a ram in the bush. He sends people to pick up were others may have left you in your life. Blood is just what it is blood but Gods connection allows you to connect with him more and spiritual fathers, mothers, brothers, and sisters. Yes, there's value in family, God created family. Don't disown or devalue it, but don't allow it to place you in bondage. When everyone has values and true understanding of the purpose of family it can be a great and successful thing.

"For ye have not received the spirit of bondage again to fear;

but ye have received the Spirit of adoption, whereby we cry,

Abba, Father.'

Roman 8:15

"Having predestined us unto the adoption of children by Jesus

Christ to himself, according to the good pleasure of his will, To

the praise of the glory of his grace, wherein he hath made us

accepted in the beloved."

Ephesians 1:5-6

Prayer

Lord you designed family. Help me to embrace my family and

not reject them, no matter how they treat me. I want to know

your purpose of family and fulfill it. Lord place agape love in

the hearts of each and every natural and spiritual family

member.

Amen

Do you struggle with family issue? Write down ways you can improve your family dynamics.

Finances

Most people go through a rough financial patch but how many people stay in that circumstance? How many makes the decision to come out of this great burden? Many can't see past their current situation and spend most of life spinning their wheels. The first thing you must do is make up in your mine that you will not settle for less because your father promised you the BEST! Second, TRUST GOD!

There was a time in my life when God was really blessing me. I had gotten married, we had our first home built, we were both working at good jobs, and expecting our first child. All these things were happening back to back then in one day our life took a turn. Three months after having our first child I was laid off from my job unexpectedly and we lost a good bit of our income. I immediately didn't understand why this God who promised me he would take care of me would allow this to happen. Things seem to go from worse to worse to worse. There were times when my daughter didn't have and our family members would show up with baby cereal, food, and water. They didn't know the extent of our situation but God used them to provide the needs of our child. A year later we were still struggling to make it and I was still having a hard time finding work. My husband got into a bad car accident while on his way to work and a few days after I discovered we were expecting our second child and I wasn't excited to find this out being that I was on birth control. So, I was feeling even more discouraged because I felt God knew we were already struggling and how were we going to take care of another child. So now, were down to one vehicle and no one working because my husband hurt his back in the accident. In the midst of this ongoing storm. God allowed my father in law to allow my husband to use a little black truck he purchased to get back and forth to work for himself. My husband went back to work and pressed his way through pain at one job, cutting yards, and delivering pizza so that we could barely make it. There were many weeks when all we had left was $20 after paying what we could pay and we used it for food for our daughter and I chose for my husband to eat before me because he needed strength. I was pregnant and went many times hungry because I felt my child needed to eat and my husband needed strength to work. In spite of, God still provided for me many times. One day I was extremely hungry and God used someone at my church to walk up to me and put money secretly in my hand and her exact words were "go get you something to eat, whatever you want" and another instance, I was hungry and I was cleaning my house and I just thought to myself, Lord all I need are some cleaning pads and some chips and soon after I received a call from someone telling me they were stopping to the store and asked what did I need. God was still with me even at my lowest. For a while I didn't understand why we were going through these hard times but I got more into the word and on my knees and God soon revealed to me why. He told me that in the beginning of my blessing I was focused on him and then I shifted away from him and so to bring me back to him he had to allow me to go through this almost rock bottom and financial set back to see him so I wouldn't be lost. It didn't stop there but things were better because we learned that no matter how low it seemed he never let us hit the bottom.

You don't have to have millions to be prosperous. Prosperity comes in many forms and it begins in the mind. Its not wanting what someone else has but being happy with what's designed for you in your lane. Satan will try to make you feel like others are living a better life than you, but don't be envious of anyone. Be happy for them because you want what God has for you and not what he has for someone else. Money is not life, some people have lots of it, some have a little, and some have none. Don't let money determine your faith, mood, and relationships.

"Beloved, I wish above all things that thou mayest prosper and be in health, even as thy soul prosperth." 3 John 1:2

Prayer

Father, you said in your word that above all things I will prosper and be in good health. Im standing on your word. Im believing that you will bless me financially with all that's for me withholding nothing. Give me the wisdom and understanding on how to spend, save, share, and invest. Give me the strength to know that you are in control and I will be alright.Lord, Thank you for the financial increase.

Amen

Vengeance

"Dearly beloved, avenge not yourselves, but rather give place unto wrath: For it is written, Vengeance is mine; I will repay, saith the Lord. Therefore, if thine enemy hunger, feed him, if he thirst, give him drink: for in so doing thou shalt heap coals of fire on his head. Be not overcome of evil, but overcome evil with good."

Roman 12: 19-21

The urge to get even can place a heavy burden on you. It tends to stop your focus on what's important and your purpose. When you're consumed with revenge and the need to prove wrong in a person, your causing yourself to go backwards and you're in sin. This scripture says it all. It's not your place to get angry and even, God knows who has wronged you so allow him to inflict the retribution. They actually cause it on their self, because you reap what you sow. We want an apology so bad when we are wronged that our belief in the word goes out the window. At one point in my life I became so tired of foolishness that I found myself angry and I wanted vengeance on all those who wronged me and I wanted God to uncover all the lies that were told, to reveal the hate, and to show their wrong. But God gave me Romans 12: 19-21 and he sent a confirming word while I was in church. The message brought forth was about vengeance and wanting God to repay and reveal. Before the scriptures and confirming word, I wanted to take things into my own hands and sometimes I wanted to physically put my hands on some individuals but I made up in my mind that I was going to look past the individual and not allow Satan to pull me into my past. God has called me to be a greater person and I made the conscious decision to be who I was called to be. THE GREATER ME! You have that opportunity as well, grab your power back. Be a better you, than get yourself dirty with retaliation.

Prayer

Lord help me to seek love and not vengeance. I don't want to sit in pity and hate. It is not my place to pay evil back with evil. Fix every need to be right rather than righteous.

Amen

Study Luke 6:20-36

"Recompense to no man evil for evil. Provide things honest in the sight of all men."

Romans 12:17

"And above all things have fervent charity among yourselves: for charity shall cover the multitude of sins."

1 Peter 4:8

Healing

Spiritual and Natural

Sickness in our bodies can absolutely be defeated. God has given us the power to call any attack to our bodies to cease. When faced with any type of sickness we tend to get off guard, we go to the store and to the doctor's office to get medicine to get well. But the God that we serve is the God of all powers and can do all things. Satan not only attacks our body, but he attacks our mind. He comes with negative thoughts for us to give up, he comes with excuse of why we can't read our bible and pray. He makes us think we are weaker than we are. The bible is full of scriptures that can and will encourage us and help us speak healing to our body and mind. The word will encourage us when we can't find physical encouragement. Fill your mind with the word of God and speak to your body. Don't allow yourself or people to speak negativity on your health or your mind.

Testimony

Satan started attacking my body at a very young age. My mother would say it was always something with me and that they stayed in the hospital with me. Im a witness that God said no, each time he planned to take my life! I went through surgeries and lots of hospital stays I beat the odds. I wrecked in a smashed totaled van and got out walking. I fought the urges to take my life as a teenager and adult. God healed by body when it felt like it was going to give out. Don't carry the weight of sickness, you have access to a God that will heal you. Satan can not have your life! It is not his to give nor take! LIVE!

"And ye shall serve the Lord your God, and he shall bless thy bread, and thy water; and I will take sickness away from the midst of thee."

Luke 8:40-56

"Heal me, O Lord, and I shall be healed; save me, and I shall be saved: for thou art my praise."

Jeremiah 17:14

Deliverance

A Dream

I opened the door of my home and a familiar face was there and immediately I charged towards her and a rage came over me and it was unrecognizable and uncontrollable. I beat this woman so bad that she couldn't move and her face was no more. The only thing that stopped me was knowing that I couldn't do any more harm to her because she was at her final breath. So, when I stood up from off this woman I recognize another person standing there that looked just like me and it begun to walk off and over to my neighbor's home and started to cause a commotion amongst the multitude of people standing there so, I followed this person that looked exactly like me and when I walked over amongst all the people I immediately started trying to convince everyone there I was the real me and the other person there was an imposter. "This is the real me, that's not me, that's not me, I am the real me!!!!" I said. All the while I'm screaming trying to convince people who the real me was the other person that looked like me never said nothing just stood there with a grin on its face. There were familiar and unfamiliar faces filling the crowd of people and they all looked at me with confused faces and said we know it's you, but there I stood still trying to convince the people. Eventually I stopped trying to convince people who already knew it was me and when I stopped the person that was imposing to look like me disappeared and immediately I felt a true happiness and peace overtake me. When I walked away from the crowd of people by the neighbor's house God forced me to fall on my face on the ground and I heard God say look up and saw two more familiar faces. They were standing away from the crowd and I heard a voice from out of the clouds say to me but there will still be some who see and think what they want. You just get up and keep moving.

This dream is an answer to a prayer of mine when I was struggling with wanting others to accept me and get to know me for who I really was and I was looking for deliverance. I prayed and asked God to show me what I need deliverance from and within a little over a week he gave me a dream. He showed me with hidden anger and no remorse in my heart and if I allowed it to fester I would eventually act on the internal rage and it would be uncontrollable and unrecognizable even to me. He also showed me fighting myself, trying and wanting people to see the real me and accept me without judgement and love me. Now everything was true because at that time I was angry at a lot of hurt, discussed with betrayals, and naturally fed up and just angry. Anything could and almost did set me off. But there was a piece of me that always made me feel that I was better than allowing it to overcome me and come out. I was reminded constantly of the scripture that says when a person is delivered and allows that same spirit entrance again it comes back seven times worse. God was giving me a glimpse of me at a point of no return. I didn't want the progress and the relationship I have with God to be destroyed, because I knew that my relationship with Christ was more important than a moment of natural satisfaction that could cause a lifetime of pain, not only to me but others. I didn't want to be lost again and not be able to get back to God, the risk was too high. But I asked God to deliver me and he delivered me from that anger and that need to want to explain myself and get everyone's approval. I was tested several times before I knew and each time I failed I continued to pray and claim deliverance until I passed the test of anger and I knew that internal hate and anger was gone. I prayed that God would take away the need of acceptance of man and replace it with the need to have his acceptance and approval. God will deliver you, there's nothing too hard for God. Keep pressing pass your fleshly desires, don't give up. Remember if God allowed you to go through it your built to overcome it with the help of the Lord.

Prayer

Lord there are some things on the inside of me that I know you are not pleased with. Forgive me father, cleanse me of all impurities, those I know not of and those that I know of, wash me Lord. Lord your word says that you are a deliverer. I believe your word to be true and I believe you are a unbiased God. A loving God you are, I ask that you deliver me and cast all unrighteous acts and sin out of my mind, body, and soul.

Amen

*Write a Deliverance Prayer

Forgiveness

One of the biggest weight's we allow to hold captivity over our true self is forgiveness. We tend to find it hard to forgive once we have given chance after chance. We boldly say, "How dare they disrespect me like this, I can't trust them. I'm done with them!" At one point in my life I thought that my forgiveness should be earned but God gave me a reality check. He's constantly giving me a word or test to put me back into perspective and spirituality.

People often say forgiveness is something that should be earn. I disagree now, forgiveness should be given freely. Why you ask, it's because we serve a God that forgives us of our sins on a constant daily basis and he's the creator of all things and has all the power. He can take life away and/or the things he has blessed us with to receive in a matter of seconds. Who are we to deny forgiveness to those that has offended or hurt us. There is power in forgiveness. There is freedom in forgiveness. If a person has offended or hurt you, whether it's emotionally or physically, FORGIVE THEM, your soul is at stake. Don't you want to be free?!

It's not up to you to fight the battle, and the battle is not with the flesh that you see in front of you, it's with the spirit on the inside of the individual. The war that is being fought is spiritual and it's important that you don't get caught up with the natural. It's only an urge to be momentarily satisfied when you attack the individual who wronged you. God has installed a wonderful power within each of us to call things into existence and the power to cast out all demons and negative things out to hurt or harm you. YOU HAVE DOMINION, YOU HAVE THE POWER!! It is not our place to judge but it is our place to be a light in darkness and show love and kindness. So, forgive because it's ultimately beneficial for you and your soul. You can't make it into heaven with ANY hate or sin on the inside and Satan knows that. So,the next time Satan tries to get you upset or in a uproar and angry with a person, quick tip to confuse the enemy. Stop, smile, and make a genuine jester of love. Don't let the enemy win because while you're not taking holding a grudge serious. The enemy knows you can't enter heaven with un-forgiveness and a grudge filled heart. He is already destined for hell, don't be in his company by allowing the minor things in life to set you up for hell. Do you want to go to heaven? Do you want peace in your life? Do you want to go higher in God? Do you want to hear God tell you well done? Then FORGIVE!!

"And be ye kind one to another, tenderhearted, forgiving one another, even as God for Christ's sake hath forgiven you."

Ephesians 4:32 KJV

-Testimony-

I was horrible when it came to forgiveness. I had the mind frame of once you cross me and I had given what I felt was enough chances I was done with you. I figured I knew who that person was and all they were about. Have you ever heard, I forgive you but I don't forget, well that was me. I didn't realize that wasn't true forgiveness and I certainly wasn't free. I remembered and sometimes wrote down what a person would do to me along with the date and time. How childish that was of me and how dare I write down the offenses of others that was done to me. I discovered that I hadn't forgiven the person. There would be times when a person I claimed I "forgave" would walked by and I felt negativity in my heart or I found myself not wanting to say hello to that individual. I had to reflect on me and Gods relationship, I had to ask myself does God hold all the wrong I've done to him and myself against me in our current relationship? The answer I got was ABSOLUTELY NOT!

"As far as the east is from the west, so far hath
he removed our transgressions from us."

Psalms 103:12

This scripture alone tells us that the sins we have committed are forgiven. I had to realize that I have no authority to hold a charge to someone. I am supposed to deal with those who has offended me with love.

Testimony

I had several altercations with a young lady at one point in my life and I wasn't saved at this time. I would go around her to taunt and tease her and I thought I was hilarious. She would do things to get under my skin also. Until one day I just was over it and I was completely tired of everything that was going on. I had made up in my mind to leave her alone and I also prayed for her and I asked God to fix it. It wasn't too far after that prayer that I was home and my sibling came to me and told me someone was at the door for me and I went to the door and this same young lady who I had all these bad altercations with was standing at my door bearing gifts and apologizing to me. Although we weren't best friends we both had peace when we were around each other and neither one of us felt any inward negativity.

Forgiveness should be REAL. You must forgive and forget, don't allow something negative to occupy space in your head. If it's there Satan uses it every time that person's name is mentioned, every time that person walks by, and every chance he gets he will use it. Before you know it your hating that person again and back where you first started, in sin. Forgiveness is truly freedom. It is your duty as a saint to truly forgive and just love, no matter what the opposer may be doing or feeling. God can handle them way better than you can.

Write your personal prayer of forgiveness.

Perception Isn't Reality

I truly don't agree with the saying "a person's past tells their future". If there was no possibility of change God would not have allowed his son Jesus to come down to this evil world and go through all he did for everyone if change wasn't possible. I'm so glad God doesn't give up on us on our first, second, third, fourth, and so on, mistake. If change wasn't possible God would not have ever sent his son, Jesus. And God has the power to end it all with a blink of the eye, but thank God for Jesus because he knows we are worth more than man say we are and more than we think we are.

I was told as a child you will never be anything, no one will ever want you, you are the swamp lady. If I allowed those words to determine who I am today I wouldn't be married to my soul-mate, I wouldn't have my beautiful children with my husband. I would be on the street or in someone's strip club allowing men to treat me any kind of way and accepting a piece of boy rather than a whole man and chasing money on drugs.

It is important that we don't judge naturally. We should ask God to take away that spirit of naturally judging someone and give me eyes to see my brother or sister with a spiritual eye and pray for them when I see they are struggling with something. When lead only by you lord give me the words to say to my brother or sister to help bring them out of their sinuation. There's a difference in judging.

(Sinuation- a situation that involves any types of sin small or large.)

"Speak not evil one of another, brethren. He that speaketh evil of his brother, and judgeth his brother, speaketh evil of the law, and judgeth the law: but if thou judge the law, thou art not a doer of the law, but judge. There is one lawgiver, who is

able to save and to destroy: who art thou that judgest

another."

James 4:11-12

Don't Move through life allowing other people's perception of you determine who you are or putting you in a box. Be who God has called you to be. When you live the life God has ordained for you and walk in your purpose the perception of others won't ever matter because your consistently being the greater called you. Rather than the natural you who changes depending on who your around. We all have a great purpose and a greater you on the inside, but we must come out of all the family curses passed down, take off the earthly labels given to you by those who hate you and the enemy, Satan, and take off the self-hate that we tend to place on ourselves.

Testimony

In one sinuation, Someone claimed to know that I am mean and short with them, not knowing that I was short(quick answered) because every time I talk with anyone in the midst of a conversation I would be talking and people would cut me off and go to another person or place their attention on the things around them. This left me feeling as if the conversation wasn't good enough therefore I felt I wasn't good enough to hold a conversation with. So, to not cause a fuss about my feeling when asked a question I would answer quickly so they could move on to the next person because I was left feeling not good enough. Now there's fault on both ends because if I was consistently the person God called me to be, the greater me that rose above rather than going low. No matter what that individual would do I wouldn't change how I handle a them, I would've shown more love and allowed God to fix the Sinuation. On the other hand, judging me and claiming to know who I was and labeling me nasty, rude, or without understanding wasn't justified. Especially, when not really knowing anything but my name was wrong and could've been handled differently. Ultimately, there was no win on either side because I shut down completely and allowed people to think/determine who they say I was. And I allowed barriers and walls to be put up. So no one showed the example of Christ, which ultimately is love and compassion.

When you don't embrace the Godly you it can be interpreted wrong and you are sub-coming to your natural flesh which ultimately reflects sin and cause people to be intimidated or earthly curious about you because they can't put their finger on what it is about you. When people are earthly curious they tend to throw titles and labels on you, which most of the time is negative and unconsciously speaking death on your life and not life into your life. God has already labeled you his and has already spoken great things and many blessings over your life since the beginning of time. It is up to you to embrace the Godly you and walk in it. People in the world will judge no matter what, just take the box of judgement and false perception and stand above those who are labeling you.

"Judge not according to the appearance, but judge righteous judgment."

John 7:24 KJV

Prayer

Lord thank you for never giving up on me and for your everlasting unconditional love. You have loved me in spite of my failures and wrong, you look past my wrong and you see the greater me. Thank You. Lord, place a hedge of protection around me, so that no man's perception of me can pierce my mind, body, or soul. Help me see great things about me daily.

Amen

Turning Victim Into Victory

Growing from Hurt

Negative words can make you feel less than and insecure. I know that's how I felt even though my outer appearance showed unphased at times, but I was inwardly insecure, full of hurt, felt unworthy, and a mess. I had battled with those feeling on and off most of my life. It's hard to know your worth, how special you are, your gifts, and value when you are told your nothing from the time you can understand. I was torn down before I could even begin life. God had to teach me that I am who he says that I am. It was a process and it's a daily walk.

There's a lesson even in hurtful situations and experiences. The lessons make you much stronger and wiser. We must take the weights caused by the enemy working against us and make it work for us. Instead of keeping the cycle of negativity going destroy the cycle with love. Stand in Godly love, honesty, and positivity to every person you encounter daily, no matter what's going on. When the choice to be better and not bitter is made you not only strengthen yourself but you are breaking chains for the next person. By stopping the negativity, that spirit doesn't travel to the next person. In negative situations turned positive God is being seen and that person sees God in your positive action. Even if a person still chooses to mistreat you or be negative, you've done what's right and they will be held responsible for their actions.

Life is not going to be all roses, but life can and will be easier with God on your side. With God on your side you must remain connected to him so that you can make the decision to rise above negativity. When choosing to be positive you are not allowing negativity in your spirit and there's less weights affecting your connection with God. You must protect your spirit. Be careful of the things you watch, speak, and allow others to speak to you about.

"Let all bitterness, and wrath, and anger, and clamour, and evil speaking, be put away from you, with all malice."

Ephesians 4:31

To get over hurt, disrespect, malice, or anything that disturbs your spirit can be very tough when you try to attack it alone. I have been in a place where I have prayed and I've seen God turn my enemies into my footstool at a young age and I didn't know any better I just knew I didn't want confusion anymore.

I've been in a place where I've prayed and I've asked God to allow a situation for me and another person to talk and he had done exactly as I asked and we talked and it was better for a while and then things went back as they were before. I've asked God to take it completely and fix as he sees fit so the problem can never return or come back up. This was the hardest for me because as I prayed that prayer and the enemy started planting seeds and stirring up even more. It left me feeling discouraged and wondering why God wouldn't resolve a matter. Instead of seeing that Satan was the culprit I found myself focused on the person and their fault. I felt like I was getting hit back to back and getting no justice to prove my righteousness. I wanted God to vindicate me and because I wanted quick result I started slowing taking the anger back on and I didn't want to deal with people. I just wanted to call them out but things seemed to get worse. When we ask God to take something give it to him and leave it there. Keep your eyes on him and getting better and your progress,he will deliver peace. It's naturally hard but God has this life of ours figured out and VICTORY BELONG TO HIM!

Even when your right in a situation don't get caught up in being right that your no longer righteous. When someone crosses you and wrong you or hurt you or even use you. Listen for that soft voice and just pray. Don't get caught up in wanting justice because you quickly sink in SIN. You will find yourself thinking ungodly things, you will find yourself getting madder and madder. All while Satan is sitting back laughing. I want you to know he's not going to stop, he has no boundaries. He wants to see you get revenge, he wants you to have anger on the inside because he knows that no sin can enter into heaven.

Keep pressing through and looking up! God's got it. When it seems as if you have no one and the world is against you- know that you are not alone and God is there. He's always with you. The older saints have a saying, "God has your back, your front, and your sides." There is no greater guard then him. Take each step in righteousness and in Jesus name. When someone comes and you know their intentions are of evil or they are coming to hurt you. Look to God, he won't allow nothing to happen if you couldn't take it. If he allows it, it's because your strong enough to endure it and he's trying to elevate you. Victory is God not yours!

*Read the story of Paul, Acts 28

"The light of the body is the eye: therefore when thine eye is single, they whole body also is full of light; but when thine eye is evil, thy body also is full of darkness. Take heed therefore

that the light which is in thee be not darkness. If thy whole body therefore be full of light, having no part dark, the whole shall be full of light, as when the bright shining of a candle doth give thee light."

Luke 11: 34-36

"Let thine eyes look right on, and let thine eyelids look straight before thee."

Proverbs 4:25

"Set a watch, O Lord, before my mouth; keep the door of my lips."

Psalms 141:3

"No weapon that is formed against thee shall proper; and every tongue that shall rise against thee in judgement thou shall condemn. This is the heritage of the servants of the Lord, and their righteousness is of me, saith the Lord."

Isaiah 54:17

Are there boxes in your way that's stopping you from being connected with God?

List Them.

Are you throwing boxes in the way of people that cross your path by choosing to allow the flesh to lead and cause negative words or actions?

Write a prayer asking God to take away those negative infirmaries and for forgiveness.

In life Satan automatically try's and throw weights on us. We don't have to carry those weights on us, but it's up to us whether we allow the weights to hold us down or build us. The power is in your hands to choose to help others around you build and not block them.Be wise about the moves you make because Satan is wise about his moves. Satan is not God and he does not know your future. He is the prince of the earth, and he knows the blood line of our sin. So, he attacks with the history of sin that runs in your family . He attacks with temptation and lust of the flesh and things of the world. That's why it's good to break those family chains. Think on heavenly things and not things of this world. He is sending his spirits out to attack you and kill you. When you find yourself longing for something out of the blue, Satan is trying to plant a seed. Don't pick it up! IT'S A TRAP FOR DISTRUCTION!! Call him out and tell him he can not tempt you because you are a child of the most high!

Read/Study Matthew 4:1-11

Prayer

Lord in the beginning of time you predestined that I be VICTORIOIOUS! Father I bind the spirit of negativity and depression. Replace the urge to retaliate with nasty words and disrespect with true love, kindness, and prayer. Lord make me better. Take away the urge to listen or speak gossip, lies, sorrow, and damnation over my brother or sister's lives. Give me a humble loving tongue. Protect my spirit Lord, your word says that no weapon formed against me will proper. I am standing on your word and I know it to be true.

Amen

Shedding The Old, Embracing The New

Past Experience

"Hey cheetah, spotted cheetah! Fat Girl!" I was called this by some of my peers every time I walked by because I had small and large black spots on my legs and I was a bit on the plump side. I was always embarrassed and ashamed. They made me feel less than and although the boys and some girls would have teased me about my appearance, there were some boys that would run by and smack my backside. I wasn't smart enough to say stop because they made me feel as if they were accepting me to a degree and in some weird way I felt as if I was a part of the cool crowd. But little did I know, that only opened the door to things getting worse in life not better nor accepted. I had opened the door to being labeled FAST and later a WHORE.

You are a gift! NEVER compromise your body for anyone to accept you. Your body is precious from your head to toe, mind, and soul. You are a prize to anyone and should be treated as such in any friendship or relationship. Being mistreated in any form should not be tolerated. Know your value.While I was dealing with peer pressure at school at home was another story. At home I was considered the lazy one and the dumb one. I was always counted out. No one ever believed in me or uplifted me. Although I'm not claiming to be the perfect child or innocent I was not raised to believe in myself or to know that I was more than nothing. At one point, I tried to take my life on two different attempts. One attempt I stole some pills from my oldest sister's dresser drawer and my mom's room and tried taking pills but it didn't work. I hadn't considered this at the time but I know now that God wouldn't allow me to go so far to take enough that would take my life. On the other attempt, I tried slitting my wrist because I was discouraged, felt alone, and unwanted and at that time a lot of girls had been doing it and I saw it on television shows and the news. I didn't want to be in this world anymore, but again God said NO!

*Take some time and think about words or some things that's holding you back and in bondage, write them down.

Before I accepted Christ in my life I only knew of one me. One who I wasn't pleased or happy with. I tricked myself and others to believe I was good, fine, and complete, which ultimately was a mask. But only did I not know I was less than naturally and more than I thought but I was only more in Christ.

As a child, teenager, and adult I spent a lot of time questioning my existence. I asked why am I here every day. I was always wondering what my purpose was. I questioned my being because I didn't feel loved or wanted by anyone and didn't know my worth. As far as I know growing up I was the "dumb one", less than everyone around me and treated as such by those around me. As a child my build up was nonexistent. I didn't have or know what self-worth or self-respect was. As a result, I battled all kinds of scars and spirits. I didn't have enough sense to know that God cared and even though it felt like no one cared I didn't acknowledge the one who did care because he died for me. I could have been like the other girls that had the mind frame to destroy their lives and overdosed on pills and died. I know now that there is something special about me and it was the blood of Jesus that protected me and the calling that I have placed on my life that kept me from destroying myself. These things made my acceptance of my true self harder to understand and acknowledge and accept. My true self was buried under a box filled with un-acceptance, negativity, and self-hate. I didn't know there was a greater and better me. The most important thing I didn't know was that I was loved unconditionally and that I could experience true unconditional love. Once I opened my heart to experience God's true love I started to uncover a me that was loving, loved, happy, caring, humble, giving, self-less, free, and at peace with so much more to discover about myself. This was the beginning of uncovering the layers of me.

Accepting Christ

For myself, I accepted Christ a year after I got married. I decided to get to know more about God for myself, with a made up mind. I wanted to know this God I was seeing around me in my leaders. At first I would sit in church service looking around and judging because it was different and unfamiliar then what I was used to. Then my looking turned into listening to the songs that were being sung, and eventually I started clapping and then listening to the words that were being spoken by my pastor and watching him on a first-hand basis live the bible and not just preach it. God blessed me to be able to witness my pastor's lifestyle on a firsthand basis. In that I discovered this Christian walk is real and it can be done.

After I truly accepted Christ, I say truly because I grew up in church, I was baptized, and everything but it was all done because I was supposed to do it rather than truly understanding what living a saved life truly meant and accepting Christ. But I started living a saved life according to my knowledge and understanding of Christ in the bible. I didn't automatically know who I truly was and truthfully, I became even more confused and frustrated.

I believe there's this misunderstanding that once you accept Christ everyone automatically accepts you and everything is all better and it's like a light switch. WRONG!! It doesn't work that way. Satan comes even harder and he's angry now because he's lost a member of his team. He's going to tempt you more and Satan is going to try everything that he can to show you that you can't change and your life before was better and its easier. He's going to throw everything at you, EVERYTHING he's ALLOWED to throw. If God allowed Satan to do it trust that you can conquer anything that comes your way.

"There hath no temptation taken you but such as is common to man: but God is faithful, who will not suffer you to be tempted above that ye are able; but will with the temptation also make a way to escape, that ye may be able to bear it."

1 Corinthians 10:13 KJV

It was with growth and understanding, by reading more and focusing more on God and spiritual things, that I began to realize I am not who my earthy father says I am, I am who my Heavenly Father says I am and there's more to me than just my name. I had begun to access my anointing and levels to the word that only God, Jesus, and the Holy Spirit could give me. I began to get a deeper relationship with Christ and realized that, everything I once knew I had to get rid of and ask the Lord to deliver me and fight my flesh with the word and deny it daily and walk in the spirit. Sounds like a lot huh? Well it's nothing compared to what Jesus did for us. He came down to show us that we can do this! Jesus was selfless by laying down his life so that we can live a holy life and make it to heaven. This life in Christ is a winning life and Satan has already been DEFEATED by Jesus Christ!! He's in misery and wants company.

You can live a holy and separated life and allow God's love to shine through you and be an example to those who are lost so that we all can make it back home to see our father and hear WELL DONE! But it wasn't until my heart was opened, that God allowed my eyes to be opened, to find out that the real me who God knew before I was in my mother's womb was not who I was told I was or who I thought I was.

I discovered my spirit man was weak the more I read and got deeper into the word and it was weak because I was full of myself and my desires was on earthly things and pleasing people around me rather than heavenly things and pleasing God.

Satan will come and put thoughts in your mind that since you've been praying and reading things are worse. I want to let you know that things were worse when you were in the world, but you couldn't see it because you were blinded by sin. In God you now have a special covering that GUARANTEE'S you safety-ness. God will carry you through whatever trial you are facing. In the world, you are not guaranteed to make it. You're playing rushing roulette with your life.

Once I discovered I was spiritually weak the battle began for me. A battle between my flesh and spirt and I could psychically feel it because I was now able to distinguish the two. My spirit man is my core which spiritually makes me naturally strong to fight against my flesh and against worldly trials, test, and tribulations, it makes me stand without wavering. It makes me keep the faith in my daily walk. It reminds me of the word, right and wrong, and it keeps me connected with God. When I sin or cloud my mind with worldly distractions my connection and spirit man is both weakened. While my flesh is momentarily satisfied.

When i'm in the flesh I can be mean, cold, hurt, guarded, angry, bitter, unapproachable, and will hold back on the basis of fear.

While when I walk in the spirit I am truly at peace, I'm able to see Satan from a distance and call him to cease. I am gentle, happy, full of love, strong, unstoppable, no man or demon can hurt me, and I am able conqueror of all things.

Almost makes you think a person is bi-polar, ha ha - but the two are totally opposites. And that's the difference in living a saved life for me versus a life lived for me and by me. A selfish life.

"Therefore if any man be in Christ, he is a new creature: old things are passed away; behold, all things are become new."

2 Corinthians 5:17 KJV

Read/Study 2 Corinthians Chapter 5

Can you imagine the two working together?......I can't.

"This I say then, Walk in the Spirit, and ye shall

not fulfil the lust of the flesh. For the flesh

lusteth against the Spirit, and the Spirit against

the flesh: and these are contrary the one to the

other: so that ye cannot do the things that ye

would."

Galatians 5:16-17 KJV

For me it was a battle, because I was persuaded I wanted to live a life for Christ and I wanted my light to shine and to make a difference and fulfill my Godly purpose. For most of my life I've felt purposeless and I now discovered real love and God had given me two things. I always wanted to be loved and to know my purpose. I wasn't giving in to the tricks of Satan, so I pressed my way. I want for people lost to find Jesus. I want the people who are lost to experience true Godly unconditional love rather than the conditional love that's given in the world. In order for that to happen the spirit must lead and not the flesh.For you to discover or continue to discover all that God has made you out of you have to begin to take those boxes that's full of weights of the world such as burdens and past hurt and destroy them. No longer allow them to hold your true self under captivity.

"And we know that all things work together for good to them that love God, to them who are the called according to his purpose."

Romans 8:28

Prayer

Lord, Help me to embrace the you in me that you have called to be. Allow me to see my wrong and let me shed those things that's not of you or accepted by you. Lord cleanse me of all anger, hurt, bitterness, and unrighteousness. Fill me with the fruits of the spirit. Forgive me for those sins I have committed knowingly and unknowingly. Lord I deny my flesh daily and ask you to fill me with your spirit, lead and guide me. Give me strength, courage, and wisdom as I walk in you daily. Bind the enemy and his tricks to steal, kill, and destroy me.

In Jesus Name,

Amen

Friendships In Christ

In my saved life, I only want to surround myself with people that's earthly and spiritually real. People with a wide range in wisdom an understanding. People that in my wrong will correct me, in my hurt and pain will pray for me and hold me up. People that will speak positive things in my life and that's vested in Christ. Someone who will hold me accountable according to the word of God and not their rules or opinion.

We tend to hang around people that's either considered below us in our eye sight or on the same level as us. I want to encourage you to embrace someone new. Don't allow Satan to plant the seed of intimidation and discard with someone that's different from you. Don't be boastful or too high- to learn from another individual. We all have great abilities and gifts in our lives, there's none great but one. The great thing about God is, he doesn't give the same gift without making it uniquely for you. God blesses each person with special gift that makes a difference and effective in its own way, only for that individual. People tend to think less than or higher than when not realizing we'll never be at the same level because what's for you is for you. No one can fulfill your purpose better than you can, BECAUSE ITS SPECIFICALLY YOURS AND YOUR NAME IS MARKED ON IT! You should only want what God has for you and go at your God given pace. As long as we all are increasing in him and moving forward we all are specially victorious.

"For we are his workmanship, created in Christ Jesus unto good works, which God hath before ordained that we should walk in them."

Ephesians 2:10

*Write down what you bring in a friendship.

*Write down what you want out of a Godly friendship

Prayer

Lord give me a heart that loves everyone, but surround me with close friends that's honest, uplifting, and friends that love you. Give me friends that will hold me accountable to your word and correct me in my wrong. Give me a heart and the wisdom to cherish my friends. Surround me with only the people you deem necessary.

Amen

Guard Your Gate

"Casting down imaginations, and every high thing that exalteth itself against the knowledge of God, and bringing into captivity every thought to the obedience of Christ."

2 Corinthians 10:5

Beware of those things and people you entertain that affects who you are, your actions, your mood, and your space. You must guard your mind, body, and soul. The enemy comes in all shapes and forms. It would be wise to surround yourself with positivity in all areas of your life.

"Be sober, be vigilant; because your adversary the devil, as a roaring lion, walketh about, seeking whom he may devour:"

1 Peter 5:8

The Mind

Satan comes to the mind and will try giving you food for thought, but you hold the power to not eat. You don't have to consume your mind with evil or foolishness. It's a trick of the enemy, to consume your mind about those things that are not of heaven. For example, If you are thinking on Susie being rude to you and all the offenses she has done to you and all the reason to validate why you feel the way you do. You are in SIN and you have no PEACE. You cannot be POSITIVE and PRODUCTIVE in mess. You have the power to say not today devil! Transform those negative thoughts to positive, uplifting, and life changing thoughts. Focus on the word of God!

No one is perfect. I've battled in my mind with negative thoughts and all the hurt people have done to me. I had to figure out that I was stagnant and consumed with hurt and offenses that others had done to me and they were living their life. I had to ask God to take control of my mind. Take away all impure thoughts and give me a mind for the kingdom. I asked God to show me my purpose and make me purpose driven, so that all I think about will be him and kingdom building.

We all struggle with things coming to our mind that take our focus off God. It may be bills, relationships, finances, and the list goes on. The key is to remain focused on God and your purpose, stay positive, and in the word of God. Don't occupy valuable space in your head with foolish things and cares of the world. When you're in commune with God and his word, it's hard for the enemy to overtake your mind. Every time he tries to come you'll be able to see him from a distance and you'll have the word and he has to flee!

Prayer

Dear God, give me peace. A peace that no man or devil can give or take or understand. Give me a mind that only thinks on you and your will. Lord take away the negative thoughts and fill me with more of you and your love. Allow my words to be uplifting and encouraging.

In Jesus Name,

Amen

"Thou wilt keep him in perfect peace, whose mind is stayed on thee: because he trusteth in thee."

Isaiah 26:3

*Study Ephesians 6: 10-24

Look To Jesus For Holiness

It's good to admire the qualities of people who have chosen to stand for Christ that you have read about or know personally. But there is only one who is good and have lead by complete example. We tend to admire people and look up to them and we place them on this pedestal and expectations on them. When they do something to disappoint us, we tend to get upset because we have set expectations on those individuals and when they fail to meet those expectations we take them out on God. We get mad with him and don't want to go to church anymore. We find ourselves not wanting to clap in church because the people whose singing doesn't deserve me clapping when we are supposed to be in the house of the Lord for God and no one else. The praise is for him not the choir or the individual singing. We stop embracing our gifts in church because man thinks little of you and is judging your every move, but our gifts are for his glory not man. You are not punishing or hurting other people or God, when you do things like this you are blocking your blessings and holding a piece of yourself captive. When did God bless you with greatness and great gifts to glorify man.... he hasn't. Everything God has given to you it's for his glory and the honor belong to him not Man.

"I will praise thee, O Lord my God, with all my heart: and I will glorify thy name forevermore."

Psalms 86: 12

Take your focus off people and take those expectations off them.

Christ came and he is the only example of perfection, he showed us that we can do this. God sacrificed his one and only son to come to this world full of sin so that you can be encouraged and know that you can make it and there's nothing too hard for God's greatest creation. YOU!

"Trust in the Lord with all thine heart; and lean not unto thine own understanding."

Proverbs 3:5

Follow Christ's steps in everything you do and when you get discouraged remember all that Jesus suffered and the persecution he went through and yet he remained faithful. Don't give up, don't give up, don't give up!

He did this for YOU!

YOU CAN DO THIS-YOU WILL MAKE IT!

God has the final say and as long as you live for him, know nothing can stop your destiny! HEAVEN!!!!!!

KNOW that God is not through with you yet. There's more in store for you, there's more growing for you to do, more of you to give, more for you to learn, more elevation! Start discovering the layers of you.

No man on earth can bless you and bless your spirit the way God can!

"The blessing of the Lord, it maketh rich, and he addeth no sorrow with it."

Proverbs 10:22

He is the only way! The only way for true peace to rule in your life.

"Jesus saith unto him, I am the way, the truth, and the life: no man cometh unto the Father, but by me."

John 14:6

Everyday choose peace! Peace in the mind, the heart, your body, and spirit!

"Let him eschew evil, and do good; let him seek peace, and ensue it."

1 Peter 3:11

Free yourself from all things Un-Godly and unrighteousness!

"Stand fast therefore in liberty wherewith Christ hath made us free, and be not entangled again with the yoke of bondage."

Galatians 5:1

Free yourself from all hurt, pain, past life and decisions.

"Remember ye not the former things, neither consider the things of old."

Isaiah 43:18

People will attempt to make you feel less than them and as if you're not worthy enough to be in their presence. They will also insist that the honor is yours in whatever you do. Most of the time if people like that wants you around its to build them up by making you feel less than. It's okay, pray for them and know your worth. Your father is the most high, so that makes you royalty. You have value and you are special.

"For I say, through the grace given unto me, to every man that is among you, not to think of himself more highly than he ought to think; but to think soberly, according as God hath dealt to every man the measure of faith."

Romans 12:3

Don't question your worth or spend time having hate towards those people. People will go the distance to make themselves feel good. Even if it's at your expense, they will go as far as lying on you to discredit who you are because of their insecurities. Don't allow a person to take your abilities and gifts and make you feel like your nothing. Satan will use other people to attack your abilities and gifts. Always be willing to see the spirit of a man and not the man. Surround yourself with people who truly cares for you with no motives and no angles.

When a person knocks you down and thinks less of you-
Take it to build up on and know that you are greater because
of he that lives on the inside of you.

"Ye are of God, little children, and have overcome them:
because greater is he that is in you, than he that is in the
world."
1 John 4:4

Ask God to put a hedge of protection around you and your
family from people and things coming to use you, break you
down, make you feel less than, from the people and things
that make you feel unworthy.

Prayer

Lord you have sent the greatest example of holiness. Help me
to look to Jesus as I continue this Christian walk. Take my eyes

and expectations off those who I see. Lord help me to focus on you and your word alone. Take away any disappointment.

Amen

Write your own personal prayer for holiness.

Tunnel Vision, No Looking Back

God has given you a great assignment and now that you've decided to be who he has called you to be Satan is mad. Satan is coming like a thief in the night, but be prepared at any moment. Be prayed up and filled with the word of God. Be prepared to be the bigger person in situations that naturally causes you to be bitter, anger, and natural minded. Be prepared to smile instead of frown when your faced with obstacles that you can't see your way out of. Be prepared to win even when it looks like you're going lose, know that you're winning. You're winning because when it's all said and done the path of righteousness that you've decided to take has built you to be even greater and the enemy is defeated. You will come out of every trial and tribulation, Better!

You can revert to your natural self quickly if you don't allow God to lead you in your everyday life. People tend to say you don't know me, referring to their past life, when in an altercation. Well, if you allow that to come out your mouth I say to you today seek deliverance. You are no longer that person from the past and if you can easily threaten a person with who you use to be than that says that there's a part of the old you still there and complete deliverance is required. The more you seek the kings face and fall into our purpose under his will. You won't even notice the attacks of the enemy because God will block it. When that is happening in your life you are being a true living example of the saying "letting God fight your battles." Stay focus on your purpose and allow all that God has made you out of to flourish and satisfy God.

"If ye then be risen with Christ, seek those things which are above, where Christ sitteth on the right hand of God. Set

your affection on things above, not on the things on the

earth."

Colossians 3:1-2

"For they that ae after the flesh do mind the things of

the flesh; but they that are after the Spirit the things of the

Spirit. For to be carnally minded is death; but to be spiritually

minded is life and peace."

Romans 8:5-6

"Rejoice in the Lord always: and again I say,

Rejoice." Philippians 4:4 KJV

List some goals you need to stay focused on:

Words Of Encouragement

You can do all that God has called you to do!

Never Give up, Press your way through.

When it looks dark and you can't see your way out continue to trust God!He didn't allow the things in your life to transpire so that you can be defeated. There's only one who has purposefully been deafeated and that's Satan. You are a Child of the KING! You will be GREAT! You will access all the gifts and blessings that God has your name on!

Be YOU, The GODLY Called YOU!

Your Gift To The World

Your past hurt, trials, and tribulations are meant to bless those you encounter in this life. You were not called here on earth to only exist. you are more than you know to be. God Loves you and because he loves you he sent you here with a gift that only you can have. You will be great and you will to come out of your situations. Your testimony on how to navigate through life's hardships will help someone. Don't give up, If you know you didn't pass the test the first time, keep pressing and with faith you will overcome your test, trials, and tribulations. All those things that the devil set out to break you and destroy you will only help build a better you! You are destined to be a victor!! It's time for you to package your gift and bless others in need of guidance and your testimony. FREE YOURSELF!!God wants you to be happy and free! Press your way through and WIN! Someone needs to be touched by your life and only you can do it! Pick up your torch and run! Don't look back, Stay focus on the Godly plan ahead, Heaven!

May   God

Bless your Life

Poems

You Are

You are worth more than you think

You are better than you think

You are more than their eyes can see

You can achieve more than those around you have told you

You are a essential piece to the kingdom and Satan will use

whoever and whatever to try and break you and stop you but

you must overcome

You must overcome the negative

you must tell the enemy he is already DEFEATED and this

battle is already won

YOU ARE A WINNER!

Who Am I

Who am I?

Does my color whether- light skin, dark skin, brown skin tell
me who I am and where I belong.

Does the length of my hair make me me?

Does the way I walk determine how you should feel about me

Does my shape whether narrow, curvy, or wide determine
who I am

When I speak you say you can tell who I am by the way I say
hello but is that true?

What if I am nervous, what if I am scared, what if I am
hurting, distraught, or in pain mentally or physically

Certainly you cant determine who I am by my hello or
goodbye

Who am i

My father said I am nothing

My mother said your just the other one

But aren't they one in the same

My friends don't know who I am because who they see is a fake me

One who pretends to satisfy the need to be accepted when im not being accepted

So.....Who am i

Tell me please, where can I get this answer

A small voice I hear says seek me, follow me, and trust me

I cant see you, who are you

But I feel you,so I'll give you a try

Just a little opening I gave and he took over completely

Who am I

I am a child of the most high

I have been marked with great qualities and gifts that are only please him but fulfills me oh so

Who am i

I am ME! A Great creation!

Full of love, peace, joy, and happiness

I am HE

My Father, My Friend, My Everything

I am He

WHAT A LIGHT

For as long as I lived I knew of one me

For as long as I lived the one me I knew was always right

But one day there was a light

A light that snuck in and overtook me

This light shine so that the one me I knew to be right I
discovered was so wrong

This light made me see my wrong and the hurt given and
received

This light forced me to reconcile with words of love and peace

Instead of the words of hate and negativity

This light condemned my wrong and made me right

This light gave me joy and an indescribable peace

This light showed me pieces of me that I've never seen

This light gave me a new opportunity

An opportunity to be free

An opportunity to truly be me

Not me that I knew me to be

But me that he knew me to be

This light made me free

What a light

What a light just for me

No Looking Back

I see darkness behind me

So I walk ahead

distraction to my left and right , what to do

I walk ahead

My past is haunting me trying to grab hold and pull me back

But with power and prayer I walk ahead

I may not see what's ahead but its lighter than what's behind
me

I may be walking without a clue but that's called faith so I
walk ahead

Faith is keeping me in light

So I walk ahead

Ahead of me is a great light, a light that shines so bright

The light is so bright I have to walk by faith because it shines

so that I can't see

But I walk ahead

What's ahead is better than what's behind

So I will continue to walk ahead

Here is a clean body, a new better you! Write the labels who you know God has called you to be:

GOD DEFINES YOU!